D1372286

My Body Does Strange Stuff!

How Do Hair and Nails Grow?

By Thomas Young

Gareth Stevens
Publishing

Please visit our website, www.garethstevens.com. For a free color catalog of all our high-quality books, call toll free 1-800-542-2595 or fax 1-877-542-2596.

Library of Congress Cataloging-in-Publication Data

Young, Thomas.
How do hair and nails grow? / by Thomas Young.
  p. cm. — (My body does strange stuff!)
Includes index.
ISBN 978-1-4824-0250-6 (pbk.)
ISBN 978-1-4824-0251-3 (6-pack)
ISBN 978-1-4824-0247-6 (library binding)
1. Hair — Juvenile literature. 2. Nails (Anatomy) — Juvenile literature. I. Title.
QM488.Y68 2014
612.7'99—dc23

Published in 2014 by
Gareth Stevens Publishing
111 East 14th Street, Suite 349
New York, NY 10003

Copyright © 2014 Gareth Stevens Publishing

Designer: Michael J. Flynn
Editor: Greg Roza

Photo credits: Cover, p. 1 Images Source/Steve Prezant/Getty Images; p. 4 iofoto/Shutterstock.com; p. 5 Blend Images/Shutterstock.com; p. 7 Mandy Godbehear/Shutterstock.com; p. 9 Deyan Georgiev/Shutterstock.com; p. 11 heromen30/Shutterstock.com; p. 13 Jayakumar/Shutterstock.com; p. 15 Lori Sparkia/Shutterstock.com; p. 17 (all) GRei/Shutterstock.com; p. 19 lenetstan/Shutterstock.com; p. 21 (boy) Zurijeta/Shutterstock.com; p. 21 (girl) Sergey Novikov/Shutterstock.com.

All rights reserved. No part of this book may be reproduced in any form without permission in writing from the publisher, except by a reviewer.

Printed in the United States of America

CPSIA compliance information: Batch #CW14GS: For further information contact Gareth Stevens, New York, New York at 1-800-542-2595.

Contents

What's Skin?. 4

Where's the Hair? 6

Get a Haircut! 10

Use Your Nails. 14

Growing Nails 16

Healthy Hair and Nails 20

Glossary. 22

For More Information 23

Index 24

Boldface words appear in the glossary.

What's Skin?

Did you know that your skin is your body's largest **organ**? It's true! Your skin keeps your insides safe. Hair, fingernails, and toenails are types of skin, too. They grow differently than regular skin because they have different jobs.

5

Where's the Hair?

Hair grows just about everywhere on the human body except for the palms and the bottom of the feet. Some people have more hair than others. Men often have thicker body hair than women. Hair may help keep the body warm when it's cold.

7

Some hair stops **germs** and dust from bothering us. Hair inside the nose traps germs and dust before they can enter your body. Your eyelashes shade your eyes from the sun. They also stop dust from bothering your eyes.

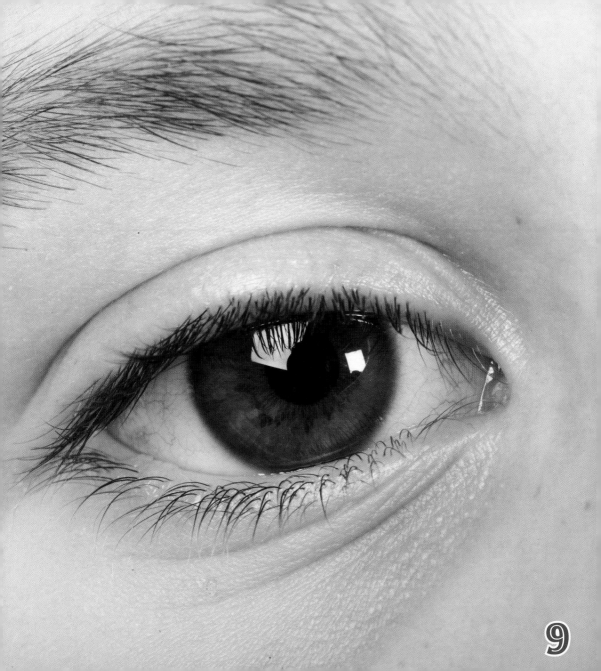

Get a Haircut!

Our skin holds many tiny hair-growing parts called follicles (FAH-lih-kuhlz). Follicles take **nutrients** from the blood and use them to grow new hair cells. The new cells push older cells out of the follicle. That's how hair grows longer!

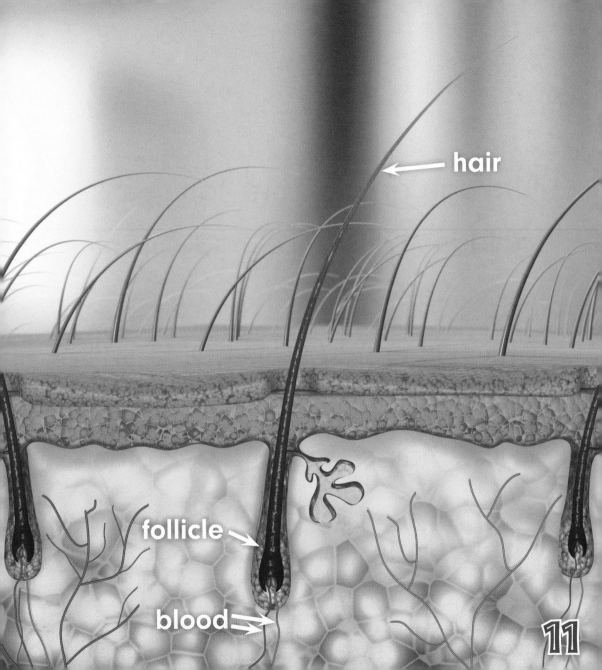

hair

follicle

blood

11

The part of a hair we can see is called the shaft. It's made up of dead hair cells. When hair cells die, they form a hard matter called keratin (KEHR-uh-tuhn). Keratin makes hair strong and **flexible**.

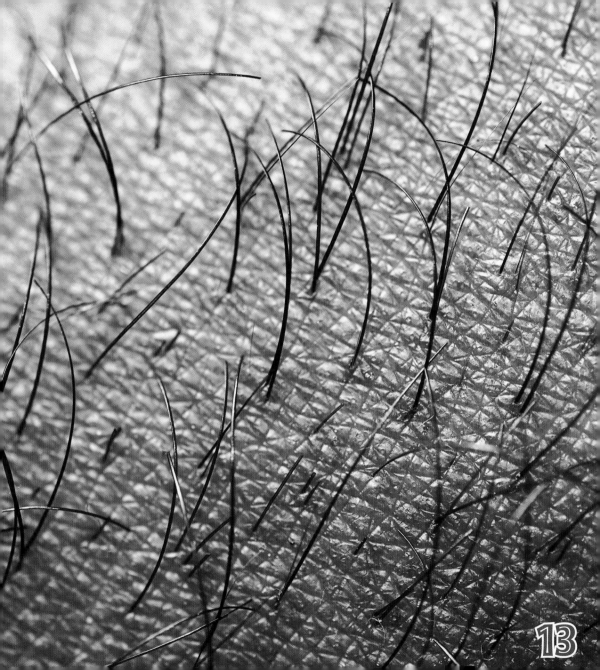

Use Your Nails

You probably know that fingernails are perfect for picking up tiny objects, such as coins. Some people believe our nails keep the ends of our fingers and toes safe from harm. However, some scientists think we don't even need our nails.

Growing Nails

Nails grow much like hair does. New nail cells form under the skin at the base of the nail. They get flattened as they grow. Together, these flattened cells form the nail plate, or the part of your nail you can see.

top view

nail
plate

side view

nail plate

17

New nail cells get nutrients from the blood. As new nail cells grow, they push older cells up. This is what makes your nails grow. Nail cells form keratin as they die. This makes our nails hard and flexible.

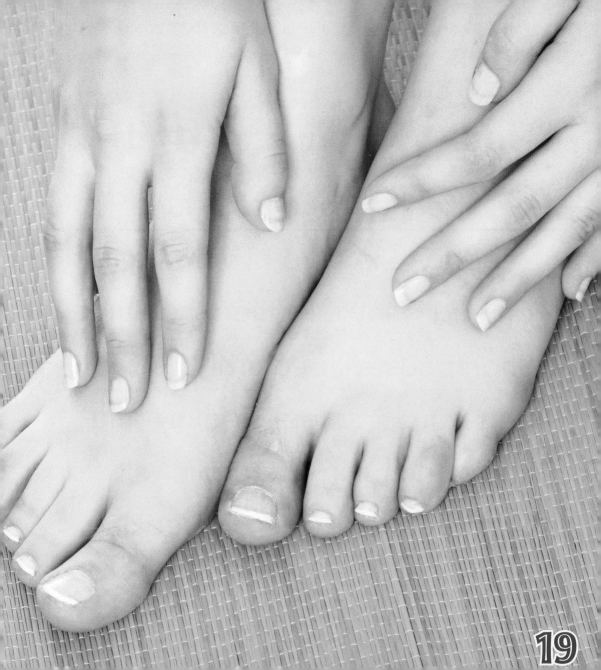

19

Healthy Hair and Nails

Just like the rest of your body, you need to take care of your hair and nails to keep them healthy. Shampoos with natural oils will help your hair look healthy and shiny. Trimming your nails will stop them from cracking or breaking.

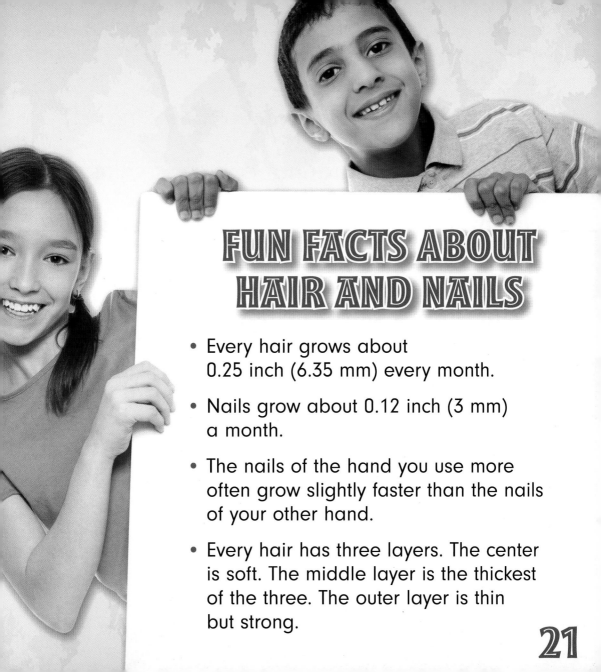

FUN FACTS ABOUT HAIR AND NAILS

- Every hair grows about 0.25 inch (6.35 mm) every month.

- Nails grow about 0.12 inch (3 mm) a month.

- The nails of the hand you use more often grow slightly faster than the nails of your other hand.

- Every hair has three layers. The center is soft. The middle layer is the thickest of the three. The outer layer is thin but strong.

21

Glossary

flexible: able to bend without breaking

germ: a tiny creature that can cause illness

nutrient: something a living thing needs to grow and stay alive

organ: a body part, such as skin or the stomach, that has a certain job

For More Information

Books

Dorling Kindersley staff. *First Human Body Encyclopedia.* New York, NY: DK Publishing, 2005.

Kenah, Katharine. *Fascinating! Human Bodies.* Greensboro, NC: Spectrum, 2013.

Websites

Your Hair
kidshealth.org/kid/htbw/hair.html
Learn more about your hair, how it grows, and how to care for it.

Your Nails
kidshealth.org/kid/htbw/your_nails.html
Read even more about your nails and how to take care of them.

Publisher's note to educators and parents: Our editors have carefully reviewed these websites to ensure that they are suitable for students. Many websites change frequently, however, and we cannot guarantee that a site's future contents will continue to meet our high standards of quality and educational value. Be advised that students should be closely supervised whenever they access the Internet.

Index

blood 10, 11, 18

body hair 6

dust 8

eyelashes 8

fingers 14

follicles 10, 11

germs 8

hair cells 10, 12

hair layers 21

healthy 20

keratin 12, 18

nail cells 16, 18

nail plate 16, 17

nose 8

nutrients 10, 18

organ 4

shaft 12

skin 4, 10, 16

toes 14